The House
with
Golden Windows

by Jenny Jinks and Shahab

D1382509

WALTHAM FOREST LIBRARIES

904 000 00682495

Once there was a rich emperor.

He lived at the top of a mountain

in a beautiful palace made of gold.

Every evening, as the sun went down,

the Emperor sat in his golden chair,

drinking from his golden cup

and eating from his golden plate.

The sun made his gold sparkle and shine.

But the Emperor was not happy.

He wanted more gold.

One evening, he noticed something
on the other side of the valley.
He could see windows sparkling
in the sunlight.
He thought they must be
made of gold.

"Golden windows," cried the Emperor.
"I want my palace to have
golden windows."
He sent for the royal builder.
"Make me windows of gold," he said.

The builder tried and tried but
he could not make windows of gold.
"I'm sorry, your highness,"
said the builder.

The Emperor was not happy.

He always got what he wanted.

Every evening, as the sun went down,

he looked at the golden windows.

"I must have that house!"

he said to himself.

So he sent a servant to find out

who owned the house and to buy it

for him.

When the servant returned,

he had bad news for the Emperor.

"I'm sorry, your highness," he said.

"The owner will not sell the house.

Not for any price."

The Emperor was very cross.

"I must meet the owner at once!"

he said.

It was a long walk all the way down the mountain, across the valley and up the other side.

By the time the Emperor had reached the top, the sun had come up.

He looked around for the house with golden windows. But all he could see was a farmer's hut.

"Where is the house

with the golden windows?"

the Emperor asked the farmer.

"Golden windows?" said the farmer.

"Do you mean the palace

on that mountain?"

The Emperor looked across the valley.
There was his palace. Its windows were
sparkling in the morning sunshine.

"I have been foolish," the Emperor said.

"I was tricked by the light."

He looked at the farmer. "I wanted to

buy your house for lots of gold.

You would have been a rich man.

Why did you say no?"

"I have my farm and my animals.
I can look across the valley at
a beautiful palace. I am happy here.
I have no need for gold," said the farmer.

The Emperor went home
to his golden palace.
He sat in his golden chair
as the sun set.
The golden windows sparkled
on the house across the valley.

"The farmer has no gold," he said
to himself. "But he is happy with
what he has."
The Emperor looked around at
all his things sparkling in the sunlight.
"It is very beautiful," he said.
And, for the first time, he felt happy
with what he had, too.

Story order

Look at these 5 pictures and captions.
Put the pictures in the right order
to retell the story.

1

The servant could not buy the house.

2

The builder could not make the windows.

3

The Emperor felt happy with what he had.

4

The Emperor wanted golden windows.

5

The Emperor met the farmer.

Guide for Independent Reading

This series is designed to provide an opportunity for your child to read on their own. These notes are written for you to help your child choose a book and to read it independently.

In school, your child's teacher will often be using reading books which have been banded to support the process of learning to read. Use the book band colour your child is reading in school to help you make a good choice. *The House with Golden Windows* is a good choice for children reading at Turquoise Band in their classroom to read independently. The aim of independent reading is to read this book with ease, so that your child enjoys the story and relates it to their own experiences.

About the book
Despite all his gold, the Emperor always wants more. Now he wants the house with golden windows he can see across the valley. But it is not for sale, and the Emperor learns to appreciate what he already has.

Before reading
Help your child to learn how to make good choices by asking:
"Why did you choose this book? Why do you think you will enjoy it?"
Look at the cover together and ask: "What do you think the story will be about?" Ask your child to think of what they already know about the story context. Then ask your child to read the title aloud.
Ask: "Do you think the house really has golden windows?"
Remind your child that they can sound out a word in syllable chunks if they get stuck.
Decide together whether your child will read the story independently or read it aloud to you.

During reading

Remind your child of what they know and what they can do independently. If reading aloud, support your child if they hesitate or ask for help by telling the word. If reading to themselves, remind your child that they can come and ask for your help if stuck.

After reading

Support comprehension by asking your child to tell you about the story. Use the story order puzzle to encourage your child to retell the story in the right sequence, in their own words. The correct sequence can be found on the next page.

Help your child think about the messages in the book that go beyond the story and ask: "Who do you think is happier – the farmer or the Emperor? Why do you think the Emperor feels happy at the end of the story?"

Give your child a chance to respond to the story: "Did you have a favourite part? What makes you feel happy?"

Extending learning

Help your child understand the story structure by using the same sentence patterning and adding different elements. "Let's make up a new story about the Emperor. What other things could the Emperor learn to be happy about? Perhaps it could be his servants or his family?" In the classroom, your child's teacher may be teaching about recognising punctuation marks. Ask your child to identify some question marks and exclamation marks in the story and then ask them to practise reading the whole sentences with appropriate expression.

Franklin Watts
First published in Great Britain in 2020
by The Watts Publishing Group

Copyright © The Watts Publishing Group 2020
All rights reserved.

Series Editors: Jackie Hamley and Melanie Palmer
Series Advisors: Dr Sue Bodman and Glen Franklin
Series Designers: Peter Scoulding and Cathryn Gilbert
A CIP catalogue record for this book is
available from the British Library.

ISBN 978 1 4451 7162 3 (hbk)
ISBN 978 1 4451 7163 0 (pbk)
ISBN 978 1 4451 7164 7 (library ebook)

Printed in China

Franklin Watts
An imprint of
Hachette Children's Group
Part of The Watts Publishing Group
Carmelite House
50 Victoria Embankment
London EC4Y 0DZ

An Hachette UK Company
www.hachette.co.uk

www.reading-champion.co.uk

FSC
www.fsc.org
MIX
Paper from
responsible sources
FSC® C104740

Answer to Story order: 4, 2, 1, 5, 3